The Way of Peace

Acknowledgments
We would like to thank all those who have given us permission to
include material in this book. Every effort has been made to trace
and acknowledge copyright holders of all the quotations in this
book. We apologize for any errors or omissions that may remain,
and would ask those concerned to contact the publishers, who will
ensure that full acknowledgment is made in the future.

The Scripture quotations used on pages 9, 19, 37, 51, 59, 71, 79,
91, 99 and 111 are from The New Revised Standard Version of the
Bible, Anglicized Edition, copyright © 1989, 1995 by the Division
of Christian Education of the National Council of the Churches of
Christ in the United States of America, and are used by permission.
All rights reserved.

Typeset in 12/15 Venetian 301
Printed and bound in Singapore

The Way of Peace

Abingdon Press

Nashville

Contents

Introduction

There are many ways of understanding and talking about peace. In the process of compiling this book, through reading, reflection and conversation with peacemakers, we have been struck by the way in which working for peace may be understood in terms of rebuilding broken community. The cessation of war is often merely the beginning – the end of a period of time that has left relationships in ruins. Wounds of betrayal and mistrust are vulnerable to the infection of what may prove to be a false peace.

We have witnessed healing of broken community in the work of such groups as the Truth and Reconciliation Commission in South Africa, the Corrymeela Community in Northern Ireland and some of the base communities of Latin America. Prayers and reflections from these and others can be found in the pages that follow.

In collecting material for this book, we contacted about seventy peace organizations around the world. We were concerned to gather material from those actively involved in situations of conflict, or in the work of peacemaking through community groups or campaigning activities. This brings a sense of realism to the prayers and reflections collected here. Some of them you may find reassuring; others may disturb. We learn that peace must be struggled for, and that this struggle is sometimes rather messy. As a brief introduction to certain pieces, we have included information about the context in which they were written, spoken or used.

It has also been clear throughout our research that the

longing and struggle for peace does not only belong to people of all religious faiths, but is close to the heart of all compassionate human beings. Whilst this is a book of prayers and reflections written and used by Christians, we do not wish to suggest that Christianity itself is the way of peace, but that it participates in the way of peace that is a human quest. The following words from Dom Helder Camara, former Archbishop of Olinda and Recife in Brazil, make this point.

> Those who choose active nonviolence – the violence of the peaceful – do not need religion or ideology to see that the earth is ruled today by powerful combines, economic, political, technocratic and military alliances. How would it be possible to beat these lords of the earth in armed combat when they have as their allies arms manufacturers and war-mongers?… The essential thing is this marvellous discovery: that all over the world, among all races, languages, religions, ideologies, there are men and women born to serve their neighbour, ready for any sacrifice if it helps to build at last a really juster and more human world. They belong in their own environment but they feel themselves to be members of the human family.

We have not included Bible texts on the theme of peace, but the chapter headings cluster around phrases from the Bible, often ones ascribed to Jesus himself. Furthermore, the positive concepts of peace expressed in this book reflect the richness of biblical insight. In Hebrew thought, peace was not simply the absence of war, but was described as a kind of 'well-being'. The word used is 'shalom', which carries within its meaning all that makes for wholeness and prosperity – things spiritual and things material. Shalom is primarily a social and relational state; it is not simply an individual sense of inner calm. Rather, shalom is something that exists between people – a state of justice, harmony and mutual well-being. It is much more, in fact, than the absence of war.

This rich meaning was carried into early Christianity, as seen in the following words from the New Testament: 'Let us then pursue all that makes for peace and mutual upbuilding.' Christians are again and again urged to promote relationships of justice and integrity, that they may become the peacemakers blessed by Jesus in the passage known as the Sermon on the Mount. Indeed, the greeting 'Peace be with you' was characteristic of him.

The inner peace of the individual is also present in the writings of the first Christians as a kind of serenity or assurance, a sense that God's strength was with them as they proclaimed the gospel, often in the face of grave danger and persecution.

Perhaps the biggest and easiest mistake to make is to treat the individual meaning (often regarded as the 'spiritual' meaning) and the social meaning of peace/ shalom as two separate matters. To do so is to betray this rich biblical tradition which urges people to regard the spiritual and social, the individual's sense of peace and the community's well-being, as one.

Finally, just as peace in the Bible involves prayer, worship, reflection, attitude and action, so we hope that these things are reflected in the pages that follow and in the use that will be made of them.

Hannah Ward and Jennifer Wild

CHAPTER I

And on Earth Peace

'*Glory to God in the highest heaven,*
    and on earth peace,
        goodwill among people!'

LUKE 2:14

Begin the day

B egin the day
by focusing
on God
as shining beauty,
radiant joy, creative power,
all-pervading love,
perfect understanding,
purity and peace.

MURIEL LESTER

Shalom

The Hebrew word for peace is 'shalom'. Shalom
is the substance of the biblical vision of one
community embracing all creation. Shalom implies
well-being and the wholeness of all life – material,
spiritual, physical, personal, corporate. Shalom is the
reality of Paradise. Shalom is eternal life in the holy
caring and sharing community of God's Spirit, the
blessing promised to Abraham for the salvation of
all the families of the earth.

God created us for shalom – he created us to abide
in harmony with his Spirit and all creation for eternity.
But shalom cannot be forced upon us against our will.
Shalom is a gift freely given that must be freely received.

HOWARD GOERINGER

The offspring of justice

In the Bible, peace and justice are never separated.
Peace is never simply the absence of war, it is the
active presence of justice. It has to do with human
fulfilment, with liberation, with wholeness, with a
meaningful life and well-being, not only for the
individual, but for the community as a whole. And
the prophet Isaiah speaks of peace as the offspring
of justice.

ALLAN BOESAK

Captivate me, Lord

Captivate me, Lord,
   to the end of my days,
wring out my heart
with your wise old Indian hands,
so that I will not forget
your justice
nor cease proclaiming
the urgent need
for humankind
to live as brothers and sisters.

JULIA ESQUIVEL, GUATEMALA

The spirit of kindness

God of the spirit of kindness,
in the glory of earth and sea and stars,
in the kaleidoscope of colour and shade and shapeliness,
in the patterns of humour and tenderness and touch,
we celebrate your generosity.

Forgive us when we forget the gift in our every breath,
the care that sustains our every moment,
that grace that can transform our every day.

Set us free from the prison of grudging hearts,
mean desires,
resentful spirits,
give us the courage to act with justice and generosity,
and draw us into love that does not calculate
or keep scores.

KATHY GALLOWAY

Life in God

It is quite clear that where our Lord is, peace reigns and anger has no place. I could see no sort of anger in God, however long I looked. Indeed, if God were to be angry but for a moment we could not live, endure, or be! Just as we owe our existence to God's everlasting might, wisdom and goodness, so by these same qualities are we kept in being. And though we wretches know from our own experience the meaning of discord and tension, we are still surrounded in every conceivable way by God's gentleness and humility, his kindness and graciousness. I saw quite clearly that our eternal friendship, our continuing life and existence is in God.

JULIAN OF NORWICH

May peace prevail

The prayer for peace promoted by the World Peace Prayer Society.

May peace prevail on earth!

WORLD PEACE PRAYER SOCIETY

Prayer for Nicaragua

Spread a big blanket
over the little country of volcanoes
that the bomber fighters may not find it
that the killer squads will not intrude
that the president of the united dead
will forget the little country.

Spread a big blanket
over the little country just four years old
that children may go to school
and even older women like myself
that coffee may be harvested
and medicines distributed
that nobody will be forgotten.

Spread a big blanket
held by all those who love that country
the Virgin Mary has a coat
and St Francis has a robe
he threw it at the feet of his rich father
and Ho Chi Minh wore a peasant'shirt like Sandino
of such cloth the blanket is woven.

Spread a big blanket
made of wishes that breathe so much tenderness
that they become prayers
to love is the word of action
that belongs to God
thus the blanket comes from God.

A dark blanket
spread to protect the hope of the poor
until the night will end
until, at last, the night will end.

CARTER HEYWARD

Deep peace

Deep peace of the running wave to you.
Deep peace of the flowing air to you.
Deep peace of the quiet earth to you.
Deep peace of the shining stars to you.
Deep peace of the Son of Peace to you.

CELTIC BLESSING

Find a way to peace

Written on 14 September 1995 as a reflection on the imagined grief of parents whose child had been murdered. This poem may be sung to the tune of 'Hyfrdol'.

No one understands the anguish,
No one knows the grief we share,
As the darkness falls around us,
No one seems to hear our prayer;
People smother us with kindness,
Then they walk away again:
Their compassion flawed by blindness
To our hurt, our fear and pain.

Life will not revert to normal,
Cannot be the same again;
God, through anger, desolation,
Find a way to peace through pain;
Lift the veil to understanding,
Offer insight to our grief:
Held so close by love and sadness,
Help this isolation cease.

Draw us back into the body
Of the ones who cannot face
All that we have seen together,
All that shatters time and space;
Frozen in the present moment,
Needing you in human form,
Hold us by their prayers and presence,
Fly with us beyond the storm.

ANDREW PRATT

Happily together

O God, save our shores from the weapons of death, our lands from the things that deny our young ones love and freedom. Let the seas of the Pacific Ocean carry messages of peace and goodwill. Turn away from our midst any unkind and brutal practices. Let each child swim and breathe the fresh air that is filled by the Holy Spirit.

O Lord Jesus, bless all who are makers of that inner peace that breaks down the barriers of hatred, and unite us with the open arms of your cross, that all the peoples of the world may live happily together.

AMANUKA HAVEA, TONGA

Pax Christi prayer for peace

O God, you are the source of life and peace.
Praised be your name for ever.
We know it is you who turns our minds to
thoughts of peace.
Hear our prayer in this time of crisis.

Your power changes hearts.
Muslims, Christians and Jews remember,
and profoundly affirm
that they are followers of the one God,
children of Abraham, brothers and sisters;
enemies begin to speak to one another;
those who were estranged join hands in friendship;
nations seek the way of peace together.

Strengthen our resolve to give witness to these truths
by the way we live.

Give to us:
understanding that puts an end to strife;
mercy that quenches hatred, and
forgiveness that overcomes vengeance.
Empower all people to live in your law of love.
Amen.

PAX CHRISTI UK

CHAPTER 2

Seek Peace and Pursue It

Depart from evil, and do good;
seek peace, and pursue it.

PSALM 34:14

Standing by one another

You are my family, an African,
   you gave me a piece of bread.
You are my friend, an Algerian,
you gave me your hand.
You are my brother, a Jew,
you helped me when trouble came my way.
And you, a Chinese, you showed me the way.
Let's stand by one another, my friends,
because you, the African,
don't have a lot of bread;
to you, the Algerian,
people don't give their hand;
people make trouble for you, the Jew;
and stand in the way of you, the Chinese.
But this bread,
this hand,
this help in trouble,
this way,
will lead us to peace.

AFFIRMATION OF PATRICE, A YOUNG FRENCHMAN

The holy compassion of God

If you love the justice of Jesus Christ
more than you fear human judgment,
then you will seek to do compassion.
Compassion means
that if I see my friend and my enemy
in equal need,
I shall help them both equally.
Justice demands
that we seek
and find the stranger,
the broken, the prisoner
and comfort them
and offer them our help.

Here lies the holy compassion of God.

MECHTHILD OF MAGDEBURG

The unity of love

O God Eternal, good beyond all that is good, fair beyond all that is fair, in whom is calmness and peace: reconcile the differences which divide us from one another and bring us back into the unity of love which may bear some likeness to your divine nature. Grant that we may be spiritually one, both within ourselves and with one another, through the grace, mercy and tenderness of your son, Jesus Christ. Amen.

AN ORTHODOX PRAYER

Hear my voice

Written on a visit to Hiroshima in 1981.

To you, Creator of nature and humanity, of truth and beauty, I pray:

Hear my voice, for it is the voice of the victims of all wars and violence among individuals and nations.

Hear my voice, for it is the voice of all children who suffer and will suffer when people put their faith in weapons and war.

Hear my voice when I beg you to instil into the hearts of all human beings the wisdom of peace, the strength of justice and the joy of fellowship.

Hear my voice, for I speak for the multitudes in every country and in every period of history who do not want war and are ready to walk the road of peace.

Hear my voice and grant insight and strength so that we may always respond to hatred with love, to injustice with total dedication to justice, to need with the sharing of self, to war with peace.

O God, hear my voice, and grant unto the world your everlasting peace.

POPE JOHN PAUL II

Wait with vigilance

We are not the guarantors of redemption. The Spirit may or may not bring our redemptive purposes to fruition in ways which we can see or measure. We often experience the forestalling and frustration of redemption. We live by faith, not by sight; by promise, not by warranty; by covenant, not by contract. The salvation promised is not for our narrow careers but for all of creation. The vision still awaits its time. And we wait with vigilance, for it will surely come.

KEN SEHESTED

Real peace

O God, teach us to distinguish
negotiation and betrayal:
when to defend our truth until the end;
and when to climb down
from our embattled certainties
in search of real peace.

JANET MORLEY

Truth is medicine

The following are some 'rules of thumb' regarding the problem of truth-telling in newly liberated societies.

1 The truth needs to be told.

2 It needs to be told completely.

3 If the threat posed by the old regime and its forces prevents full disclosure, then as much should be revealed as is possible.

4 The truth needs to be sanctioned by an official body. If the new government is too weak to do it, then it should be done by the churches.

5 At least the leading architects and executors of the policy of disappearances, murder and torture should be prosecuted.

6 If they cannot be prosecuted, they should at least be publicly exposed.

7 Amnesty should not be offered until the truth has been told and, if possible, at least some of those most guilty prosecuted.

In sum, a society recovering from the trauma of state violence needs as much truth as possible. Truth is medicine. Without it, a society remains infected with past evils that will inevitably break out in the future.

WALTER WINK

Love, joy and peace

This poem may be sung to the tunes of 'Tallis Canon' (verses 1, 3 and 5) and 'Morning Hymn' (verses 2, 4, 6 and 7).

How can we sing a Song of Peace
when all God loves is scorched by war?
How dare we now confess our faith,
when guarded by things we deplore?

Because we sing of peaceful means,
outmatching all that violates,
of ways of peace so well expressed
in all the Christian celebrates!

How can we sing a Song of Joy
where victims over victims mourn?
How dare we here maintain our hope
where right is wronged and wholeness torn?

Because we sing the joyful truth
that violent ways are obsolete,
that Gentle Jesus has the wit
to make God's purposes complete!

How can we sing a Song of Love
while disregard and hatreds last?
How dare we claim a future life
while murderous ways are far from past?

Because we sing Love's new-found tune
(by discord-makers much despised)
of rights restored and wrongs forgiven,
Creation safely harmonized.

We gladly sing: Love, Joy and Peace!
We hope to God that wars may cease!
We celebrate: Christ is The Way,
The Truth and Life... for all... today!

DAVID J. HARDING

A prayer for continued peace in Ireland

The following two prayers were compiled by Pax Christi UK for St Patrick's Day, 17 March 1998.

Lord Jesus Christ,
You are the way of peace,
Come into the brokenness of this land
With your healing love.
Help us to be willing to bow before you
In true repentance
And to bow to one another
In real forgiveness.
By the fire of your Holy Spirit
Melt our hard hearts and consume
The pride and prejudice
Which separate us from each other.
Fill us, O Lord, with your perfect love
Which casts out fear
And bind us together in that unity
Which you share with the Father
And the Holy Spirit for ever. Amen.

PAX CHRISTI UK

The Lord's Prayer

Adapted out of the 'troubles' in Northern Ireland.

Our Father, who art in Heaven, hallowed be thy name. Thy Kingdom come. Thy will be done, on earth as it is in Heaven. Give us this day our daily bread. And forgive our trespasses, as we have forgiven those who trespass against us. For if we haven't, there isn't much point going any further. But if we have then we dare ask for two great favours: to be delivered from all evil and to learn to live together in peace. Go naofar D'aninm. For thine is the Kingdom, the Power and the Glory for ever and ever. Amen.

PAX CHRISTI UK

A crescendo of dialogue

Written in 1964 on the author's installation as Archbishop of Olinda and Recife, Brazil.

It is essential to begin,
trustingly,
a crescendo of dialogue.
It would be a grave matter
before the judgment of God and of history
to withdraw oneself
from the reconstruction of the world.

DOM HELDER CAMARA

Central American Lord's Prayer

Our Father
who is in us here on earth
holy is your name
in the hungry who share your bread and your song.
Your Kingdom come,
a generous land where confidence and truth reign.
Let us do your will
being a cool breeze for those who sweat.
You are giving us your daily bread
when we manage to get back our lands
or to get a fairer wage.
Forgive us for keeping silent in the face of injustice
and for burying our dreams.
Don't let us fall into the temptation
of taking up the same arms as the enemy.
But deliver us from the evil that disunites us.

UNKNOWN

Prayer for peace in Natal

Hear us, Lord, as we pray to you.

We pray for those within the violence, that your spirit of peace may descend and put an end to the forces of violence. Let there be true peace, not brought about by domination, oppression or the barrel of a gun, but by a change of heart.

We pray for the victims of violence, that through a commitment to peace and reconciliation their needs for food, shelter and protection may be met. For those who have lost family, we pray that they find comfort in their suffering and that they not seek vengeance.

We pray for ourselves as the Church and South Africans, that we may have courage; that we may not be apathetic and just look on but overcome separation and complacency; that we may be moved to share ourselves in prayer, time and effort; that we may not only blame others but see the flaws in ourselves that cause the sickness in society, and that we may be moved to witness to the truth.

We pray, also, for those in the world who suffer in the same way.

Let us not forget your love, power and compassion. Let us hope as Mary and Martha hoped for Lazarus: that, as at Easter, there may be resurrection of life, love and hope.

We ask these things, heavenly Father, in the name of your Son, Jesus, knowing that, in faith, they will be granted. Amen.

UNKNOWN

A prayer for all those involved in reconciliation

The Corrymeela Community in Northern Ireland is committed to, and works for, peace and reconciliation in that land. This is their Members' Prayer (said together).

God, we believe that you have called us together to broaden our experience of you and of each other. We believe that we have been called to help in healing the wounds of society and in reconciling people to each other and to God. Help us, as individuals or together, to work, in love, for peace, and never to lose heart. We commit ourselves to each other – in joy and sorrow. We commit ourselves to all who share our belief in reconciliation – to support and stand by them. We commit ourselves to the way of peace – in thought and deed. We commit ourselves to you – as our guide and friend.

CORRYMEELA COMMUNITY

Choose life, choose love

This poem/hymn was written on 6 July 1985 for the Choose Life Conference in Uppsala and sent to us by the Christian Peace Conference of the Czech Republic.

Choose life, choose love – the hour is late!
Say 'yes' to Christ and 'no' to fate.
Join hands with people of the faith,
reach out in hope to all who live.

In seeking space and life for each,
we need to practise what we preach,
to turn into creative deeds
the inner urges of our creeds.

With Christ-the-Least, renouncing power,
we face the challenge of this hour,
we rise against the death of earth,
the end of life, the end of birth.

The hour is late! Choose life, choose love,
with Christ into God's future move:
life to the full, the earth a feast,
through making, speaking, being peace.

FRED KAAN

Liberator of the oppressed

Throughout the Bible God appears as the liberator of the oppressed. He is not neutral. He does not attempt to reconcile Moses and Pharaoh, to reconcile the Hebrew slaves with their Egyptian oppressors or to reconcile the Jewish people with any of their later oppressors. Oppression is sin and it cannot be compromised with, it must be done away with. God takes sides with the oppressed. As we read in Psalm 103:6, 'God, who does what is right, is always on the side of the oppressed.'

FROM THE KAIROS DOCUMENT, SOUTH AFRICA

Vulnerable God

Vulnerable God,
    you challenge the powers that rule this world
through the needy, the compassionate,
and those who are filled with longing.
Make us hunger and thirst to see right prevail,
and single-minded in seeking peace;
that we may see your face
and be satisfied in you,
through Jesus Christ, Amen.

JANET MORLEY

Peace, justice and solidarity

Christ taught us that our neighbourhood is universal: so loving our neighbour has global dimensions. It demands fair international trading policies, decent treatment of refugees, support for the UN and control of the arms trade. Solidarity with our neighbour is also about the promotion of equality of rights and equality of opportunities; hence we must oppose all forms of discrimination and racism... We claim whatever rights and opportunities are available to us only in order to exercise an influence on behalf of whatever we believe to be true and good, especially in solidarity with people everywhere who are on low incomes, disabled, ill or infirm, homeless or poorly housed, in prison, refugees or who are otherwise vulnerable, powerless and at a disadvantage.

THE COMMON GOOD: STATEMENT OF CATHOLIC BISHOPS'
CONFERENCE OF ENGLAND AND WALES

Woman

Woman, in a dark and quiet corner of the home, patient, resigned, waiting for this sublime hour in which a just revolution would break her yoke and untie her wings.

ANA BETANCOURT, CUBA

CHAPTER 3

The Things that Make for Peace

As [Jesus] came near and saw [Jerusalem], he wept over it,
saying, 'If you, even you, had only recognized on this day
the things that make for peace! But now they are hidden
from your eyes.'

LUKE 19:41–42

Painting peace

I had a paint box
but it didn't have the colour red
for the blood of the wounded,
nor white
for the hearts and faces of the dead.

It didn't have yellow either
for the burning sands of the desert.

Instead it had orange
for the dawn and the sunset
and blue
for new skies
and pink
for the dreams of young people.

I sat down and painted peace.

TEN-YEAR-OLD, LATIN AMERICA

Beyond self-knowledge

They tell about a man who took great pride in his lawn, only to wake up one day and find a large crop of dandelions. He tried every method he knew to get rid of them. Still they plagued him. Finally, he wrote to the Department of Agriculture. He enumerated all the things he had tried and closed his letter with the question, 'What shall I do now?' In a few weeks the reply came: 'We suggest you learn to love them.'

MARY LOU KOWMACKI

Assurance of pardon

Christ is our peace;
those who are divided
he has made one.
He has broken down the barriers of separation
by his death and he has built us up
into one body, with God.
To whomsoever repents and believes
he has promised reconciliation.
So, live as people reconciled.
Amen.

UNITED CONGREGATIONAL CHURCH OF SOUTHERN AFRICA

Reaching out to God during these difficult times

Did you hear the latest tragic news over the radio? A dead body was found buried in a shallow grave, most probably a 'salvage' victim. O God, when will the institutionalized violence end?

There was also the report of another encounter between the military and the rebels, both sides suffering casualties. More people dead. The military operations continue to intensify, and increasing numbers of families have to leave their homes. Who says that there has been an end to strategic hamletting* in Mindanao?

The newscaster reported on the prices of basic commodities in the market. The housewives are groaning. Then about the workers of a plywood factory going on strike. There is police harassment at the picket lines. The workers are raging. The bad news goes on and on. One gets numb with all the suffering, pain and anguish that lie behind the news stories.

We are living in difficult times. Where is God, and how does one reach him? He has promised to be his people's protector, but it seems like he has abandoned them.

In the midst of a bleak scenario, one echoes the same lamentations expressed in the Psalms: Lord, do not abandon us. Show us your mercy. Let justice roll down like the waters. Show us your righteousness. Remember your covenant with the people. Listen to our cry!

*forced removal of families from their homes to an unknown location

Although there are times when we feel ourselves to be light years distant from the Lord, we also find ourselves, at certain moments, to be in the palm of God's hand. Reaching out to God can be both a frustrating experience and an encounter of faith and hope. Sometimes God is unreachable. Other times he is right there in our midst.

When we reach out to a brother in need of friendship, or a sister in need of comfort, we encounter God. We see his face in the face of the person in need of help and are reminded of our kinship with each other in God's name. The peasant's face, the widow's anguish and tears, the detainee's blank gaze – these are God's faces. One embraces them and finds that God is in one's arms.

It is during these times of rage and hope for the coming of liberation that God, in fact, makes us experience an emptying so that we are ready to take into our hearts the poor and oppressed.

Direct our steps, O Lord, into the way of justice and peace.

EDITH NATIVIDAD, PHILIPPINES

Sea of Galilee

*The peaceful waters of the Sea of Galilee form a vast
natural reservoir. Water is taken in a conduit right down
to the Negev, in order that the desert should 'blossom as
a rose'. How water use is to be controlled and shared is
crucial to any final peace agreement. While Palestinian
water supplies have been restricted, Israeli farmers and
settlers have enjoyed subsidized rates for water, and have
used it disproportionately. Overuse is leading to serious
problems like the salination of drinking water in Gaza.*

This is your peace:
the water gently slapping on the stones;
soft hills, cool churches,
a sunset to dream about,
that moment of stillness at the lake's heart.

This is your peace:
these waters fairly shared
in a thirsty land –
crops that flourish,
children who drink
without fear of disease –
waters whose sweetness and abundance
are lasting signs of your grace.
Blessed are those who hunger and thirst
    after righteousness,
for they shall be satisfied.

JANET MORLEY

Private and public lives

A comment on the Peace Prayer of Hindu origin (see below) made famous by Mother Teresa of Calcutta.

It is the only prayer that I know that links private and public lives. It was used to help the United Nations Special Disarmament Programme in 1982. Mother Teresa was in St James's Church, Piccadilly, introducing it, and her words were, 'When I gave some rice to somebody who hadn't had any for months, that lady gave it to somebody else.' That, she said, is neighbourliness, that is peace. So I see it as linking the personal and the public. There was a very public person saying 'peace is right between me and my next door neighbour', especially the sick and poor person.

DONALD SWANN

Lead me from death to life,
From falsehood to truth;
Lead me from despair to hope,
From fear to trust;
Lead me from hate to love,
From war to peace;
Let peace fill our hearts,
Our world,
Our universe.

HINDU PRAYER

I realize again

I realize again
that troubled wrongfulness
is
not so much
the willingness to bomb
as
unwillingness to talk
is
not so much
the willingness to make war
as
unwillingness to make peace
is
not so much
the ability to lie
as
inability to tell the truth
is
not so much
the ability to doubt
as
inability to believe
is
not so much
the readiness to hurt
as
unreadiness to heal

is
not so much
the readiness to hate
as
unreadiness to love
is
not so much
doing
as
undoing
by
not doing.

Cursed
are these
who
will not make
peace;
war shall be made
for them.

DAVID J. HARDING

Who will speak
my words now?

*Milton López is a five-year-old Nicaraguan who was
seriously injured by a Contra mortar attack.*

Who will speak my words now
and ask my questions?

I have no words to tell my story,
but there must be a way to make the world listen,
even though I am five years old
and speak only Spanish –
if I could speak,
but I am missing half my jaw.

Who will speak my words now
and ask my questions?

My family is poor,
and with those who were starving
went to cut coffee in the mountains,
where fighting began before I was born.

The scream of mortars was not known to us
before I fell slower than the rest –
but not as slow as the fire against my face.

Who will speak my words now
and ask my questions?

When was the decision made
that I would never shout with joy or anger
and sing psalms in church
or disturb the priest's homily?
What were you thinking when you fired the shells,
when you shipped the weapons,
and when you signed the order that destroyed
all the words I want to speak,
all the questions I need to ask?

I am not a story.
I am not a debate.
I am a prayer.

Who will speak my words now
and ask my questions?

AMAYA LÓPEZ (MILTON'S MOTHER), NICARAGUA

Prayer rosary

Hiroshima,
Bosnia,
Belfast,
the names slip
through our fingers,
like bloodstained beads.

As we tell the story,
tell us,
tell us,
tell us
the way to peace.

Saigon,
Sarajevo,
Rwanda,
still they come,
countless numbers:
people hounded,
refugees tramping the road
out of hell, into hell.

Where will it stop?
Show us,
show us,
show us
the way to peace.

Five for sorrow,
ten for joy,
may what has been
sown in pain
be reaped in hope.

KATE McILHAGGA

Nonviolence

Nonviolence is not for the élite few, it is for everyone to live, it is a way of life based on respect for each human person, and for the environment.

It is also a means of bringing about social and political change, and resisting evil without entering into evil.

It is a whole new way of thinking.

MAIREAD MAGUIRE, NORTHERN IRELAND

Show us the peace

Show us, good Lord,
the peace we should seek,
the peace we must give,
the peace we can keep,
the peace we must forgo,
and the peace you have given us
in Jesus our Lord.

UNKNOWN

CHAPTER 4

Not as the World Gives

'Peace I leave with you; my peace I give to you. I do not give to you as the world gives. Do not let your hearts be troubled, and do not let them be afraid.'

JOHN 14:27

Shalom: vision and reality

Israel was given the vision and promise of shalom. At times the vision faded and the promise was forgotten as century followed century from Abraham to Moses, to David, to Nehemiah. But there were always the Jeremiahs to remind Israel of God's promised shalom:

'I will fulfil to you my promise and bring you back to this place. For I know the plans I have for you, says the Lord, plans for shalom, and not for evil, to give you a future and a hope' (Jeremiah 29:10–11).

Old Testament visions of shalom finally became New Testament reality of shalom in the God-Person who could say what no other lips have ever dared to say:

'Shalom I leave with you; my shalom I give to you; not as the world gives peace do I give to you' (John 14:27).

HOWARD GOERINGER

Decisiveness

Christ, who is whole, wants us whole. He loves decisiveness. He loves his enemies more than his half-hearted friends. He hates his falsifiers more than his opposites. What he abhors is the lukewarm, the colourless grey, the twilight, the foggy, pious talking that mixes everything up and commits one to nothing. He sweeps all that away whenever he draws near.

EBERHARD ARNOLD

A new sign of peace

O God,
you bring hope out of emptiness
energy out of fear
new life out of grief and loss.
As Mary returned to mourn
yet found unspeakable joy,
so comfort all who have lost their homes
through persecution, war, exile,
or deliberate destruction.
Give them security, a place to live,
and neighbours they trust
to be, with them,
a new sign of peace to the world.

JANET MORLEY

The dove

One olive tree above the flood
and one branch is the sign
of solid land again.
You bring hope, messenger of peace.

What olive leaves do we discover
in the world's flood of pain?

The fall of a dictator,
a pact between old enemies,
a government halving its spending on arms,
a family embracing different cultures,
a doctor's care in a war-torn land,
and children with uncorrupted eyes.

Jesus of the olive grove
you knew the agony of doubt.
Shall we be saved?
Yes, in the garden dawn;
yes, in the upper room
and yes, where the tree of life
bears leaves to heal the nations.

BERNARD THOROGOOD

Come, wage peace with us!

Text of a poster for new members of the Baptist Peace Fellowship of North America.

Peace plans its strategy and encircles the enemy.
Peace marshals its forces and storms the gates.
Peace gathers its weapons and pierces the defence.
Peace, like war, is waged.
But Christ has turned it all around:
the weapons of peace are love, joy, goodness,
    longsuffering,
the arms of peace are justice, truth, patience, prayer.
The strategy of peace brings safety, welfare, happiness,
the forces of peace are the sons and daughters of God.
Peace, like war, is waged.

WALKER L. KNIGHT

Come, Holy Spirit

*From a liturgy of repentance and rededication to peacemaking
for the Fellowship of Reconciliation in England, 1992.*

Spirit of blessings, shine on our company
Spirit of darkness, weave in us your new creation
Spirit of weakness, empower us
Spirit of justice, challenge us
Spirit of peace, make us the messengers of your peace.
Spirit of the Living God who makes all things new,
Holy Spirit, come!

MARY ANN EBERT

Give thy peace

O peaceful King of peace, Jesus Christ, give unto
us thy peace, and confirm unto us thy peace, and
forgive us our sins, so that we may be worthy to come
and go in peace.

ETHIOPIAN LITURGY

Silent before God

We constantly need the crucified Christ within us. To receive him we must become silent before God again and again. Christ wants to live in our hearts so that we are able to conquer all things. Through him everything receives its true meaning. There is no other foundation for true peace of heart than unity with him. Only Christ can bring us to full trust in God. In him we find the sharpest judgment of wrath over all evil, but also the revelation of his loving grace.

J. HEINRICH ARNOLD

The Lord's majesty

Can any praise be worthy of the Lord's majesty? How magnificent his strength! How inscrutable his wisdom! Man is one of your creatures, Lord, and his instinct is to praise you… The thought of you stirs him so deeply that he cannot be content unless he praises you, because you made us for yourself and our hearts find no peace until they rest in you.

AUGUSTINE OF HIPPO

Prayer at the beginning of the day

O Lord, let me greet the coming day in peace. Help me in everything to rely on your holy will. In every hour of the day reveal your will to me. Bless my dealings with all who surround me. Teach me to treat all that comes to me throughout the day with peace of soul, and with firm conviction that your will governs everything. In all my deeds and words guide my thoughts and feelings. In unforeseen events let me not forget that all are sent by you. Teach me to act firmly and wisely, without embittering and embarrassing others. Give me strength to bear the fatigue of the coming day with all that it shall bring. Direct my will, teach me to pray, pray you yourself in me.

PHILARET OF MOSCOW

All the day long

May he support us all the day long, till the shades lengthen, and evening comes, and the busy world is hushed, and the fever of life is over and our work here is done! Then in his mercy may he give us a safe lodging, and a holy rest, and peace at the last.

JOHN HENRY NEWMAN

CHAPTER 5

Swords into Ploughshares

For out of Zion shall go forth instruction,
    and the word of the Lord from Jerusalem.
He shall judge between the nations,
    and shall arbitrate for many peoples;
they shall beat their swords into ploughshares,
    and their spears into pruning-hooks;
nation shall not lift up sword against nation,
    neither shall they learn war any more.

Isaiah 2:3b–4

Make your circle, God

Make your circle around the poor,
God of love;
make your circle around the hungry,
God of compassion;
make your circle around the oppressed,
God of liberation;
make your circle around the victims of war,
God of peace.

JOHN JOHANSEN-BERG

A new world

Eternal God
We confess to you our sinfulness.
You made the world a paradise
but we have turned our lands into
places of tears and unhappiness.

People are fighting with each other
race against race.
The holocaust of chauvinism
sweeps through countries
devouring humanity
terrorizing us into submission.

Liberating One
free us from all bondage
so that our faith in you
will make us free
to create with courage
a new world –
new societies.

UNKNOWN, SRI LANKA

May anger and fear turn to love

Written by a white lay person who joined black workers in resisting the bulldozing of their shacks. Nkwenkwe Nkomo was one of thousands of young people jailed without trial during the era of apartheid in South Africa.

O God
whose Son in anger
drove the money-changers
from the temple
let the anger of Nkwenkwe Nkomo
and his fellow detainees
be to the cleansing
of this land.

O God
I hold before you
the anger
the rage
the frustration
the sorrow
of Mrs Nkomo and all black mothers
who demand for their children
the same chance to grow up
strong and tall
loving and unafraid
as any white mother
wants for her children;

in penitence
I offer you
my own mixed-up anger
that it, with theirs,
may be taken up
into your redemptive will

in which the clash
between anger and fear
oppressed and oppressor
can give way
to the incomprehensible action
of agape-love
bringing about the reconciliation
the embrace of the other
the alien
the enemy
creating the festival of shalom
in which the wolf shall lie down
with the lamb
and the whole of life on earth
shall rejoice
in the splendour of your glory.

MARGARET NASH

A North American prayer

Our God,
We have made you over a thousand times
in our image:
a machismo God,
desperate for superiority,
anxious for homage,
dominating,
a sensuous god,
adoring riches,
devouring possessions,
extravagant,
a national god,
flexing muscles,
subduing nations,
untouchable,
a tribal deity,
who mocks the power of gentleness,
the strength of weakness,
the victory of surrender.
Forgive us, our God,
for worshipping images
of our brokenness,
not yours.

Forgive us, our God,
for fearing
the broken God on the cross,
poor, frail, agonizing, triumphant.
Smash our idols, opulent, warlike,
restless deities
who bear no resemblance
to our brother, Jesus Christ.

Our God,
make us over,
a thousand times,
endlessly,
in your image.

MARY HAMMOND, OHIO

A prayer for help when arguments get out of hand

When our love is torn or battered,
When relationships are strained;
When all sense is broken, scattered,
And our draught of care is drained;
Cool our tempers, give us patience
And a willingness to wait,
Ears to listen, clearer vision,
Ways of hope instead of hate.

When our anger breeds resentment
And our words are filled with spite;
When we cannot find contentment,
Doing wrong, avoiding right;
Still our storming, raging, rending,
Quell our striving, help us cease
All this pleading and pretending;
Show us truth and bring us peace.

ANDREW PRATT

Hand in hand

It is a joy when hundreds of women
march hand in hand with the message
   of peace and nonviolence.
Men spend millions of rupees to manufacture
   war materials
while millions of people die from hunger.
We need women to stop this.
We need to liberate and educate women.

BEENA SEBASTIAN, INDIA

God is not far from my people

God is not far from my people
hidden in a corner,
nor could you believe he tires
of hearing so many praises
pleading for his salvation.

God is God, not like humans:
he opens both his hands
to those seeking his love;
he weeps together with his people
when they die tortured
as his son once died.

Many good people are dying
in following those good steps
which Jesus showed us.

They are tortured and trampled
because they lived the gospel
and gave the people their love;

Because they told that Jesus Christ
will come as King from heaven
to bring a better government.

All those who have died
will be woken anew
through the grace of the Lord.

There will be justice in the towns
and repression will be no more.

Today his people sing a prayer,
with so much love
we praise him in our heart.

God is here with his people,
he is here with us.
God is here and in his name
we ask for his peace to reign.

HENRY BRAN

Like Aaron's staff

May your peace be ours from the day
we cause justice to bloom
like Aaron's staff.

PABLO GALDÁMEZ, EL SALVADOR

CHAPTER 6

When there is no Peace

For from the least to the greatest of them,
    everyone is greedy for unjust gain;
and from prophet to priest,
    everyone deals falsely.
They have treated the wound of my people carelessly,
    saying 'Peace, peace',
    when there is no peace.

JEREMIAH 6:13–14

Say no to peace

Say 'No' to peace,
if what they mean by peace
is the quiet misery of hunger,
the frozen stillness of fear,
the silence of broken spirits,
the unborn hopes of the oppressed.

Tell them that peace
is the shouting of children at play,
the babble of tongues set free,
the thunder of dancing feet,
and a father's voice singing.

Say 'No' to peace,
if what they mean by peace
is a rampart of gleaming missiles,
the arming of distant wars,
money at ease in its castle,
and grateful poor at the gate.

Tell them that peace
is the hauling down of flags,
the forging of guns into ploughs,
the giving of fields to the landless,
and hunger a fading dream.

BRIAN WREN

Nobody's business

One of the most persistent ambiguities we face is that everybody talks about peace as a goal, but among the wielders of power peace is practically nobody's business. Many men cry 'Peace! Peace!' but they refuse to do the things that make for peace.

The large power blocs talk passionately of pursuing peace while expanding defence budgets that already bulge, enlarging already awesome armies and devising ever more devastating weapons…

Before it is too late, we must narrow the gaping chasm between our proclamations of peace and our lowly deeds which precipitate and perpetuate war. We are called upon to look up from the quagmire of military programmes and defence commitments and read the warnings on history's signposts.

One day we must come to see that peace is not merely a distant goal that we seek but a means by which we arrive at that goal. We must pursue peaceful ends through peaceful means. How much longer must we play at deadly war games before we heed the plaintive pleas of the unnumbered dead and maimed of past wars?

Martin Luther King, Jr

In place of a curse

At the next vacancy for God, if I am elected,
I shall forgive last the delicately wounded
who, having been slugged no harder than
 anyone else,
never got up again, neither to fight back,
nor to finger their jaws in painful admiration.

Those who are wholly broken, and those in whom
mercy is understanding, I shall embrace at once
and lead to pillows in heaven. But those who are
the meek by trade, baiting the best of their betters
with the extortions of a mock-helplessness
I shall take last to love, and never wholly.

Let them all into Heaven – I shall abolish Hell –
but let it be read over them as they enter:
'Beware the calculations of the meek, who
 gambled nothing,
gave nothing, and could never receive enough.'

UNKNOWN

Talk to us

Talk to us about reconciliation
only if you first experience
the anger of our dying.

Talk to us of reconciliation
if your living is not the cause
of our dying.

Talk to us about reconciliation
only if your words are not products of your
    devious scheme
to silence our struggle for freedom.

Talk to us about reconciliation
only if your intention is not to entrench yourself
more on your throne.

Talk to us about reconciliation
only if you cease to appropriate all the symbols
and meanings of our struggle.

J. CABAZARES

Poem of an angry person

Because we eat roots
And flour piles up in your warehouses…
Because we live all cramped up
And your space is so abundant…
So we are not allies.

Because we are soiled
And you are shiny bright…
Because we feel suffocated
And you lock the door…
So we distrust you.

Because we are abandoned on the streets
And you own all the shade…
Because we endure floods
And you party on pleasure boats…
So we don't like you.

Because we are silenced
And you never stop nagging…
Because we are threatened
And you use violence against us…
So we say to you NO.

Because we may not choose
And you are free to make plans…
Because we have only sandals
And you are free to use rifles…
Because we must be polite
And you have jails…
So NO and NO to you.

Because we are the current of the river
And you are the stones without heart…
So the water will erode away the stones.

W.S. RENDRA, INDONESIA

Peace that passes understanding

Risen Jesus,
we thank you for your greeting,
'Peace be with you'.
The shalom of God, deep lasting peace;
peace that brings inner calm;
that keeps a person steady in the storm;
that faces the persecutor without fear
and proclaims the good news with courage
and with joy.
This is the peace that reconciles
sister to brother, black to white,
rich and poor, young and old;
but not a peace that is quiet
in the face of oppression and injustice.
This is peace with God,
the peace that passes understanding.

JOHN JOHANSEN-BERG

CHAPTER 7

Not Peace but a Sword

'Do not think that I have come to bring peace to the earth;
I have not come to bring peace, but a sword.'

MATTHEW 10:34

Peace and conflict

*Quoted from a review of a book by the sociologist
David Martin.*

He assumes Christianity is only about reconciliation
and peace: I think conflict is also near its heart.

HUGH MONTEFIORE

Peace in the fight

I call it an illusion for Christians to seek peace, as
though the gospel wanted to make life comfortable
for them. The contrary is true. 'I came not to bring
peace but a sword.' As long as the fight is going on,
we have peace only in the fight. Our peace is not a
well-being; it is a participation in Christ...

C.F. BLUMHARDT

Cleansing the temple

*This poem may be sung as a hymn, to the tune of 'Ewing'
or 'Aurelia'.*

Is this the gentle Jesus
Whose healing touch is balm,
Consoler of the broken
And messenger of calm?
Is this the friend of children
At whom the tempests cease –
Are these his hands of blessing,
Is this his voice of peace?

His eye is bright with anger,
His workman's arm strikes clear –
The traders cringe and scatter,
Torn by unholy fear.
The mighty temple totters,
For all its golden wealth:
The Spirit blows a tempest
Of cleansing, of new health.

This is the day he promised
Of good news to the poor –
Cast out the old corruption
That blocks the temple door!
Throw wide the gate of freedom,
Let all God's children come! –
Through Jesus' broken body
God's people shall come home.

MARY ANN EBERT

A new heart

Lord Jesus,
you experienced in person
torture and death
as a prisoner of conscience.
You were beaten and flogged,
and sentenced to an agonizing death
though you had done no wrong.
Be now with prisoners of conscience
throughout the world.
Be with them in their fear and loneliness,
in the agony of physical and mental torture,
and in the face of execution and death.
Stretch out your hands in power
to break their chains.
Be merciful to the oppressor and the torturer,
and place a new heart within them.
Forgive all injustice in our lives,
and transform us to be
instruments of your peace,
for by your wounds we are healed.

UNKNOWN

Why have you forsaken me?

Lord, O Lord my God
why have you forsaken me?
I am a caricature of a man
people think I am dirt
they mock me in all the papers.

I am encircled:
there are tanks all around me
machine-gunners have me in their sights:
there is barbed wire about me –
electrified wire.
I am on a list
I am called all day
they have tattooed me
and marked me with a number.
They have photographed me behind the barbed wire
all my bones can be counted
as on an X-ray film.
They have stripped me of my identity
They have led me naked to the gas-chamber
They have shared out my clothes and my shoes.

ERNESTO CARDENAL

Your peace

Come Lord,
do not smile and say
you are already with us.
Millions do not know you,
and to us who do,
what is the difference?
What is the point of your presence
if our lives do not alter?
Change our lives,
shatter our complacency.
Make your word our life's purpose.
Take away the quietness
of a clear conscience.
Press us uncomfortably.
For only thus
that other peace is made,
your peace.

DOM HELDER CAMARA

Armed struggle

Daniel, a former university student, wrote in June 1986 of why he joined the guerrilla movement in El Salvador.

My faith led me to join the armed struggle. I believe that God loves the poor. That is why I felt my Christian duty was to witness to the teachings of Christ. One Gospel text, Matthew 25, has always been particularly important to me. The Lord asks how we can love God – whom we do not see – and not love our brother or sister whom we see every day. I came to the conclusion that faith must be expressed in love for our brothers and sisters, particularly the poor and the oppressed. In El Salvador there is no way to escape this conclusion: the gospel leads to a total commitment to the revolutionary struggle.

DANIEL, EL SALVADOR

Witness of the women

Christ, whose bitter agony
was watched from afar by women:
enable us to follow the example
of their persistent love;
that, being steadfast in the face of horror,
we may also know the place of resurrection,
in your name, Amen.

JANET MORLEY

World of contradictions

This poem may be sung as a hymn, to the tune of 'St Clement'.

O God of peace, your beauty calls us
　　While conflicts rage and cares dismay:
How can we smile when love impels us
To strive and bleed to end the fray?

When healing flees as pain consumes us
Or pity fires our angry eyes,
How dare an opening leaf beguile us
Or birdsong taunt the thundery skies?

How dare you, God, assault our grieving
With tender buds and radiant stars?
The gossamer grass and pearly sunset
Make mock of justice's call to arms.

You set before us calm and beauty,
Truth, justice, mercy — where is peace?
How can we choose when torn by tension
When blessings soothe while hates increase?

Creator God, your gift of freedom
Reveals you trust us; come what may
We walk this world of contradictions
In steadfast anguish, Jesus' way.

MARY ANN EBERT

Peace, justice and love of God

That love of others, that care for their freedom is what causes us to go into such controversial subjects as the individual and the state, war and peace. The implications of the gospel, teaching the works of mercy, lead us into conflict with the powers of this world. Our love of God is a consuming fire. It is a fearful thing to fall into the hands of the living God. It is a living God and a living faith that we are trying to express. We are called to be holy, that is, whole human beings, in this life of ours.

DOROTHY DAY

A harsh and dreadful thing

Love in action is a harsh and dreadful thing
compared to love in dreams.

DOROTHY DAY

Dedication

One day
I would like to take
Both my hands
(For I consider life
    itself too dear to lose)
Dip them in petrol
Then set them alight
With a candle flame
And dedicate them
To those who acted
While I wept and wrote.

MAHMOOD JAMAL, PAKISTAN

CHAPTER 8

The Peace of God

*Do not worry about anything, but in everything by prayer
and supplication with thanksgiving let your requests be made
known to God. And the peace of God, which surpasses all
understanding, will guard your hearts and your minds in
Christ Jesus.*

PHILIPPIANS 4:6–7

God is love

A name is not,
cannot, must not be
a label stuck
on persons or on things.

The name comes from within
the things and persons
and must on no account ring false.

It has to express
the essence of the essence,
the real reason
for the being, the existence
of the thing or person named.

Your name
is and only can be
Love.

DOM HELDER CAMARA

Fear not, stand firm

Can you imagine a general saying to his troops, 'Today we're not going to fire a single weapon. We're going to stay right where we are and not even talk. We're going to be still and pray, and God will fight for us.' The man's crazy! Must be battle fatigue.

That's exactly what the people of Israel thought when Moses was leading them out of Egypt. Looking back at the pursuing armies of Pharaoh that had them hemmed in on every side, they shouted to Moses, 'Better for us to go back into slavery in Egypt than die here in the wilderness.' Then they heard the words that would be branded permanently on the consciousness of this Covenant People: 'Fear not, stand firm, and see the salvation of the Lord, which he will work for you today. The Lord will fight for you, and you have only to be still' (Exodus 14:13,14).

HOWARD GOERINGER

The power of hope

Nailed to a cross because you would not
compromise on your convictions.
Nailed to a cross because you would not
bow down before insolent might.
My Saviour, you were laughed at,
derided, bullied, and spat upon
but with unbroken spirit,
Liberator God, you died.

Many young lives are sacrificed
because they will not bend;
many young people in prison
for following your lead.
Daily, you are crucified
my Saviour, you are sacrificed
in prison cells and torture rooms
of cruel and ruthless powers.

The promise of resurrection
the power of hope it holds,
and the vision of a just new order
you proclaimed that first Easter morning.
Therefore, dear Saviour, we can affirm
that although bodies are mutilated and broken,
the spirit refuses submission.
Your voice will never be silenced,
Great Liberating God.

ARUNA GNANADASON, INDIA

Peace beyond understanding

'Then the peace of God, which is beyond our understanding, will keep guard over your hearts and your thoughts, in Christ Jesus' (Philippians 4:7).

O Lord God, grant us your Spirit, that we may comprehend your peace. As we pray, help us to recognize what must come from you alone, for you are mighty and holy and your will is peace on earth. Your will is peace beyond all understanding, your peace in heaven and on earth and under the earth, your peace that opposes all sin and death and takes away every evil that can be named. We await you, O Lord our God, and you will hear us. No matter how long the battle lasts, we will hold out in patience, for we are your children. We shall never lose the faith that your name shall be honoured and that all things shall come in harmony with your will of peace on earth, your peace. Amen.

C.F. BLUMHARDT

A Christmas meditation

For unto us a child is born, here in our suffering. Unto us a son is given, here in our fear and despair. He is King above all the lords. His name is holy and shall be called:

The Prince of Peace – that peace which is completely different from the peace which is being enforced upon us with destructive weapons.

He is the King who is opening the doors bolted with fear, with his victorious shalom.

He is sending us into the world with this shalom, to liberate humanity from fear, to break down the walls of division and animosity and to proclaim visibly the reconciliation for which he died on the cross.

He will let his light of hope shine on all who are sitting in the darkness of despair and in the shadow of death.

And even if I die today, that will not prevent the rising of the sun tomorrow. Our hope in our Lord is greater than the fear of death.

For God loved us so dearly and embraced us with his Son, our liberator, whom he sent into our suffering, so that he could shine like the sun in all his glory and expel the night of despair, fear and death.

ZEPHANIA KAMEETA, NAMIBIA

And the waters will flow from your altar, Lord

And the waters will flow from your altar, Lord
And flood the earth.
And we will be like a garden watered,
cared for,
exposed to life.

Oh! let these waters come,
Impetuous and pure,
and destroy the powers
and clean the paths
which my people will take,
which my people will take,
singing and rejoicing
in an endless celebration,
the Word, Life, Freedom
and the Resurrection!

And the waters will flow from your altar, Lord,
and clean away the debris
and we will have courage to act,
to serve,
to change the world.

And the waters will flow from your altar, Lord,
life will be rekindled,
And we will see the new creation,
act,
of your love.

SIMEI MONTEIRO, BRAZIL

False paths

Some want to talk exclusively about the peace of their own soul or the peace they share with one another. They are incapable of representing the whole peace of God that belongs to the final Kingdom. They remain sunk in narrow-minded folly, bogged down in the swamp of isolation. But it is the same with those friends of peace who make the opposite mistake and speak about world peace without peace with God and without the social justice of complete community. They want 'pacifism' without fighting the spirits of unpeace, without battling the covetous nature of mammon, without opposing the spiritual warfare against unfaithfulness and impurity. Both of these false paths in life represent unpeace that comes from folly and indifference to all-embracing truth.

EBERHARD ARNOLD

CHAPTER 9

Blessed are the Peacemakers

'Blessed are the peacemakers, for they will be called children of God.'

MATTHEW 5:9

An instrument of your peace

Lord, make me an instrument of your peace.
Where there is hatred, let me sow love;
Where there is injury, pardon;
Where there is discord, union;
Where there is doubt, faith;
Where there is despair, hope;
Where there is darkness, light;
Where there is sadness, joy;
For your mercy and your truth's sake.

PRAYER OF ST FRANCIS

In a small way

This is for me the heart of nonviolence: that in the resistance or the demonstrations or the work against injustice you actually are beginning to act out in a small way the vision you have of a new society.

ANITA KROMBERG, SOUTH AFRICA

My peace I give unto you

Blessed are the eyes that see
The things that you have seen,
Blessed are the feet that walk
The ways where you have been.

Blessed are the eyes that see
The Agony of God,
Blessed are the feet that tread
The paths his feet have trod.

Blessed are the souls that solve
The paradox of Pain,
And find the path that, piercing it,
Leads through to Peace again.

G.A. STUDDERT KENNEDY

Look with compassion

O Lord, by whose cross all enmity is ended,
all walls of separation broken down:
look with compassion upon the agonies
    of your world,
and by the power of your Spirit
make us instruments of your peace;
you who are our peace,
now and for ever.

UNKNOWN, AUSTRALIA

Glorious opportunities

O God, we thank you for the
glorious opportunities
to build new societies
of peace, justice and love
to praise and glorify you.
Help us, we pray,
to stand up with courage,
to work with love
and to live in hope
for Christ's sake.

UNKNOWN

The will to be free

I will lift up my eyes,
from the dark night of despair,
to the dawning of my commitment to freedom.

For I cannot be forced to submit
my hopes to perpetual slavery.

Behold, they who define their freedom
in the struggle for justice
cannot be deprived of it
by the principalities and powers of this world.

The people's will to be free
is our unshakeable support;
neither intimidation nor force of arms
can destroy it.

The power of human love
struggling to transform and to celebrate all of creation
testifies that goodness and freedom
shall ultimately prevail.

CANAAN BANANA, ZIMBABWE

Women of this day

A 19th-century celebration of Mothers' Day, 'a time for women and children to speak for the things that make for peace', by the author of the 'Battle Hymn of the Republic'.

Arise, then, women of this day!
Arise, all women who have hearts,
whether your baptism be that of water or of tears!

Say firmly: 'We will not have great questions
decided by irrelevant agencies,
our husbands shall not come to us,
reeking with carnage, for caresses and applause.
Our sons shall not be taken from us to unlearn
all that we have been able to teach them
of charity, mercy and patience.
We women of one country will be too tender
of those of another country to allow
our sons to be trained to injure theirs.'

From the bosom of the devastated earth a voice
goes up with our own; it says, 'Disarm, disarm!'
Blood does not wipe out dishonour,
nor violence indicate possession…

JULIA WARD HOWE

A paraphrase of the Beatitudes

How liberated are those who have learnt to let go –
They shall experience the mystery of God.

How strong are those who are not afraid to admit
  their weaknesses –
Their tears shall heal their grief.

How beautiful are those who reverence life –
The earth shall rejoice in their presence.

How satisfied are those who seek to serve God –
For God shall be their delight.

How happy are those who are willing to forgive others –
They shall find release from guilt and fear.

How enlightened are those who know oneness with
  all things –
They shall see God everywhere.

What an inspiration are those who work for justice
  and peace –
For they shall live as children of God.

What an opportunity there is for those who suffer
  in the cause of right –
For their rejection can become the doorway to new life.

BILL WALLACE, NEW ZEALAND

Courage to stand up

Give us courage, Lord, to stand up and be counted,
to stand up for those who cannot stand up
  for themselves,
to stand up for ourselves when it is needful for
  us to do so.
Let us fear nothing more than we fear you,
let us love nothing more than we love you,
for thus we shall fear nothing also.
Let us have no other God before you,
whether nation or party or state or church.
Let us seek no other peace
but the peace which is yours
and make us its instruments,
opening our eyes and our ears and our hearts,
so that we should know always
what work of peace we may do for you.

ALAN PATON

The peacemaker's job

The job of the peacemaker is:
  to stop war,
to purify the world,
to get it saved from poverty and riches,
to heal the sick,
to comfort the sad,
to wake up those who have not yet found God,
to create joy and beauty wherever you go,
to find God in everything and in everyone.

MURIEL LESTER

Dedication of
a peace person

I have a simple message for the world from this Movement for peace.

I want to live and love and build a just and peaceful society.

I want for children, as I want for myself, life at home, at work and at play to be a life of joy and peace.

I recognize that to build such a life demands of me dedication, hard work and courage.

I recognize that there are many problems in my society which are a source of conflict and violence.

I recognize that every bullet fired and every exploding bomb makes that work more difficult.

I reject the use of the bomb and the bullet and all the techniques of violence.

I dedicate myself to working with my neighbours, near and far, day in and day out, to building that peaceful society in which the tragedies we have known are a bad memory and a continuing warning.

MAIREAD MAGUIRE, NORTHERN IRELAND

Step by stumbling step

Peace is not simply an absence of armed conflict.
Peace is not simply an absence of conflict.
Peace is not simply an absence of arms.
Peace is not simply an absence.
Peace is not simply.
Peace is not.
Peace is.
Peace.

ELIZABETH BIRTLES

Working for justice

Fill us with your Spirit
that we may follow Jesus
in all we do or say,
working for justice and bringing your peace
to this world that you have made.

UNKNOWN

Take... and make

Take our hatreds: make them into handshakes
Take our prejudices: make them into peace-offerings
Take our arguments: make them into alliances
Take our battles: make them into bonds
Take our misunderstandings: make them into music
Take our divisions: make them into dances
Take our schisms: make them into songs.

KATE COMPSTON

CHAPTER 10

And Peace will be with Us

Grace, mercy, and peace will be with us from God the Father and from Jesus Christ, the Father's Son, in truth and love.

2 JOHN 1:3

Be born in us

A lien
  strange
    distant
      separated

you are the hope of community

rejected
    abandoned
        alone
            in distress

you are the hope of love

come – abandoned alien
    God of hope

be born in us

SUE BRITTION

Web of peace

Peace is like a gossamer –
vulnerable, yet indestructible:
tear it, and it will be rewoven.
Peace does not despair.
Begin to weave a web of peace:
start in the centre
and make peace with yourself
and your God.
Take the thread outwards
and build peace within your family, your community
– and in the circle of those you find it hard to like.
Then stretch your concern
into all the world.
Weave a web of peace
and do not despair.
Love is the warp in the fabric of life:
truth is the weft:
care and integrity together –
vulnerable,
but ultimately
indestructible.
Together,
they spell peace…

KATE COMPSTON

Lord of peace

Lord Jesus, we look to you on the throne beside your Father in heaven and ask that you be Lord of peace in our hearts. Help us to overcome ourselves again and again and to remain at peace. Then your will may be done in your disciples, a power of peace may be around us that goes out into the whole world, and your name may be glorified on earth. For you are Lord of peace, and we await you. In difficult times faith and hope will take hold in our hearts all the more firmly, to your glory, Lord Jesus. For you will suddenly come according to your promise as the one who does God's will on earth among all people. Amen.

C.F. BLUMHARDT

Embrace

Let there be, in some place,
a community of men, women, elderly,
children and newborn babies,
as a first fruit, as our appetizer,
and an embrace of the future.

RUBEM A. ALVES, SÃO PAULO

'I beg to differ'

A candle-light is a protest at midnight.
It is a non-conformist.
It says to the darkness,
'I beg to differ'.

SAMUEL RAYAN, INDIA

The shadow of the dove

When dawn's ribbon of glory around the
world returns
and the earth emerges from sleep –

May the shadow of the dove be seen
as she flies across moor and city.
Over the warm breast of the earth she skims,
her shadow falling on the watcher in the tower,
the refugee in the ditch,
the weary soldier at the gate.

May the shadow of peace
fall across the all-night sitting of a council
across the tense negotiators around a table.

May the shadow of hope
be cast across the bars of a hostage cell
filling with momentary light
rooms tense with conflict,
bringing a brief respite,
a slither of gold across the dark.

May she fly untiring across flooded fields,
across a city divided by hate and fear,
across a town wreathed in smoke.

May the shadow of reconciliation,
the dove of peace with healing in her wings,
be felt and seen and turned towards
as she makes righteousness shine like the dawn,
the justice of her cause like the noonday sun.

Holy Spirit of love
bring healing, bring peace.

KATE MCILHAGGA

Outstretched hands

From his speech on receiving the Nobel Peace Prize.

B ecause of our faith in Christ and in humankind, we must apply our efforts to the construction of a more just and human world. And I want to declare emphatically: such a world is possible. To create this new society, we must present outstretched, friendly hands, without hatred, without rancour — even as we show great determination, never wavering in the defence of truth and justice. Because we know that seeds are not sown with clenched fists. To sow we must open our hands.

ADOLPHO PÉREZ ESQUIVEL

Gifts

We face each other
across a raw divide.
The chasm of our anger
filled with the bones
of old hatreds.

The wounded earth
spews out our greed
in acrid smoke.
The gaping world cries out in pain.

The upward surge of birds in flight,
wheeling and dancing
in the sun,
the sound of geese
strung across an empty sky,
the scent of blossom on the wind,
gifts of a generous Creator,
to lift, to call, to heal.

KATE MCILHAGGA

God is weaving

God is crying.
The tapestry of creation
that she wove with such joy
is mutilated, torn,
made into pieces,
its beauty worn apart with violence.

God is crying.
But see!
She is gathering the pieces
to weave something new.

She collects
the pieces from hard work;
the aim: to defend
the initiative for peace,
the protests against injustice,
everything that seems
small and weak;
words and deeds given
as sacrifice
in hope,
in belief,
in love.

And see!
She is weaving them together
with the golden threads of joy
to a new tapestry:
a creation richer, more beautiful
than the old!

God is weaving,
patient, persistent,
with a smile
that is shimmering like a rainbow
over her face, striped with tears.

And she invites us
not only to continue
to give her
our works
and our suffering pieces —

But even more —
to sit beside her
at the loom of Jubilee
and weave
together with her
the tapestry of a New Creation.

M. RIENSTRA, TRANSLATED BY YVONNE DAHLIN

Psalm 23

The Lord is my shepherd;
I have everything I need.
He lets me see a country of justice and peace
and directs my steps towards his land.

He gives me new power.
He guides me in the paths of victory,
as he has promised.

Even if a full-scale violent confrontation breaks out
I will not be afraid, Lord,
if you are with me.
Your shepherd's power and love protect me.

You prepare for me my freedom,
where all my enemies can see it;
you welcome me as an honoured guest
and fill my cup with righteousness and peace.

I know that your goodness and love will
be with me all my life;
and your liberating love will be my home
as long as I live.

ZEPHANIA KAMEETA, NAMIBIA

The sending forth

Spirit of tempest and flood, of growth, life and healing, blow through us.

In the name of Jesus, the risk-taker and liberator, who calls us by our names,

May we read the signs of the times.

May we choose with wisdom where to direct our energies, yet with willingness to suffer.

May we affirm and encourage each other in sisterhood and brotherhood, respecting each other's beliefs and honouring each other's words and actions, recognizing each other's truth.

May the trusting, sharing, suffering, rejoicing, uncontainable love which we find within the very nature of Being embrace us and send us forth.

MARY ANN EBERT

Acknowledgments

Chapter 1

1. 'Begin the day' from *Ambassador of Reconciliation. A Muriel Lester Reader*, Richard Deats (ed.), Philadelphia: New Society Publishers, 1991. Used by permission.

2. 'Shalom' from *He Is Our Peace: Meditations on Christian Nonviolence*, from *The Writings of Howard Goeringer, Eberhard Arnold, Christoph F. Blumhardt, & Others*, ed. Emmy Barth (Plough Publishing House, 1994).

3. 'The offspring of justice' quoted in *Gathered for Life*, Report of the VI Assembly of the World Council of Churches 1983 (Geneva: WCC, 1983).

4. 'Captivate me, Lord', excerpted from 'Confession' in *Threatened with Resurrection: Prayers and Poems from an Exiled Guatemalan* by Julia Esquivel, second edition. Copyright © 1982, 1994 Brethren Press, Elgin, IL 60120. Reprinted by permission.

5. 'The spirit of kindness' by Kathy Galloway, from *The Pattern of Our Days: Liturgies and Resources for Worship*. The Iona Community (Wild Goose Publications, Glasgow, 1996). Used by permission.

6. 'Life in God' translated by Joyce Blackwell in *Transcendence: Prayers of People of Faith*, ed. Daniel Faivre (London: Westminster Interfaith, 1994).

7. 'May peace prevail', World Peace Prayer Society, New York, USA.

8. 'Prayer for Nicaragua' in *Revolutionary Forgiveness: Feminist Reflections on Nicaragua*, by the Amanecida Collective, ed. Carter Heyward and Anne Gilson (Maryknoll NY: Orbis Books, 1987). Used by permission.

10. 'No one understands the anguish', Andrew Pratt © 1997 Stainer & Bell Ltd, London, England, from *Blinded by the Dazzle*. Used by permission.

11. 'Happily together' from *Your Will Be Done* (Singapore: CCA, 1984).

12. 'Pax Christi Prayer for Peace', Pax Christi British Section, St Josephs, Watford Way, Hendon, London NW4 4TY. Used by permission.

Chapter 2

1. 'Standing by one another', Universal Church, DEFAP, France.

2. 'The holy compassion of God', reprinted with permission from *Meditations with Mechtild of Magdeburg*, by Sue Woodruff, copyright 1982, Bear & Co., Santa Fe, NM.

3. 'The unity of love' from *Your Will Be Done* (Singapore: CCA, 1984).

4. 'Hear my voice', taken from *Prayers for Pilgrims* by John Johansen-Berg, published and copyright 1993 by Darton Longman and Todd Ltd and used by permission of the publishers.

5. 'Wait with vigilance' from Ken Sehested, 'Not by Might: A Meditation on the Use of Power and the Nature of our Partisanship', *Baptist Peacemaker* (Summer 1997).

6. 'Real peace' in *Companions of God: Praying for Peace in the Holy Land*, Christian Aid/Janet Morley 1994. Used by permission.

7. 'Truth is medicine', from Walter Wink, *Healing a Nation's Wounds: Reconciliation on the Road to Democracy* (Uppsala: Life and Peace Institute, 1997).

8. 'Love, joy and peace' © David J. Harding, Peace Care, 39 Halsdon Road, Exmouth, Devon EX8 1SR, England. Used by permission.

9. 'A Prayer for Continued Peace in Ireland', Pax Christi Irish Section, 52 Lower Rathmines Road, Dublin 6 Ireland. Used by permission.

10. 'The Lord's Prayer', Pax Christi Irish Section, 52 Lower Rathmines Road, Dublin 6 Ireland. Used by permission.

11. 'A crescendo of dialogue', taken from *Into Your Hands* by Dom Helder Camara, published and copyright 1987 by Darton Longman and Todd Ltd and used by permission of the publishers.

12. 'Central American Lord's Prayer' in *Praying for a Change: A Christian Aid Lent Course*, Christian Aid 1996. Used by permission.

13. 'Prayer for peace in Natal' from *Peace: A Worship Kit*, published by Diakonia, Durban, South Africa, as part of a 'Focus on Peace', Christmas 1990. Used by permission.

14. 'A prayer for all those involved in reconciliation' from *Celebrating Together*, Corrymeela Press, Corrymeela House, 8 Upper Crescent, Belfast BT7 1NT. Used by permission.

15. 'Choose life, choose love' by Fred Kaan, *Planting Trees and Sowing Seeds: 23 New Hymns* (Oxford: OUP).

16. 'Liberator of the oppressed' from the Kairos Document from South Africa, published in the UK by the Catholic Institute for International Relations and the British Council of Churches.

17. 'Vulnerable God' from *All Desires Known*, copyright © Janet Morley 1988, 1992. Reproduced by permission of SPCK and Morehouse Publishing, Harrisburg, PA.

19. 'Woman' by Ana Betancourt in *All a We a One: A Caribbean Scrapbook*, by David P. Young. © 1993 by Friendship Press, Inc. Originally published in 'Songs of the Kingdom,' by Alvin and Pauline Schutmatt, *A.D. Magazine*, April 1982. Used by permission.

Chapter 3

1. 'Painting peace' in *Lifelines: Words and Pictures for Prayer and Reflection*, Christian Aid. Used by permission.

2. 'Beyond self-knowledge' from Mary Lou Kowmacki, 'The Doorway to Peace: A Spirituality of Nonviolence' (Pax Christi USA).

3. 'Assurance of pardon' from the 24th Assembly Closing Service of the United Congregational Church of Southern Africa, 2 October 1990. Used by permission.

4. 'Reaching out to God during these difficult times' from *Your Will Be Done* (Singapore: CCA, 1984). Used by permission.

5. 'Sea of Galilee' in *Companions of God: Praying for Peace in the Holy Land*, Christian Aid/Janet Morley 1994. Used by permission.

6. 'Private and public lives', Donald Swann, interviewed by James Whitbourn for *Prayer for the Day* (BBC Radio 4); see James Whitbourn, *A Prayer in the Life* (London: Triangle, 1993).

7. 'I realize again' © David J. Harding, Peace Care, 39 Halsdon Road, Exmouth, Devon EX8 1SR, England. Used by permission.

8. 'Who will speak my words now?' by Amaya Lopez, Nicaragua from *Gifts of Many Cultures*, page 159. Used by permission of The Pilgrim Press, Cleveland, Ohio, USA.

9. 'Prayer rosary' by Kate McIlhagga from *Textures of Tomorrow: Words and Images on the Theme of Reconciliation*, ed. Kate Compston (London: URC, 1996). Used by permission.

10. 'Nonviolence', published by the International Fellowship of Reconciliation in support of its 'Culture of Nonviolence Programme'.

11. 'Show us the peace' in *Contemporary Prayers for Public Worship*, ed. Caryl Micklem, SCM Press 1967, page 48. Used by permission.

Chapter 4

1. 'Shalom: vision and reality' from *He Is Our Peace: Meditations on Christian Nonviolence*, from *The Writings of Howard Goeringer, Eberhard Arnold, Christoph F. Blumhardt, & Others*, ed. Emmy Barth (Plough Publishing House, 1994).
2. 'Decisiveness' from *Salt and Light: Talks and Writings on the Sermon on the Mount* (Rifton NY: Plough, 1967).
3. 'A new sign of peace' in *Companions of God: Praying for Peace in the Holy Land*, Christian Aid/Janet Morley 1994. Used by permission.
4. 'The dove' from *Leaves from the Tree of Peace: A Resource Book of Words and Pictures*, ed. John P. Reardon. Published by the United Reformed Church © 1986. Used by permission.
5. 'Come, wage peace with us!' by Walker L. Knight. Used by permission.
6. 'Come, Holy Spirit' © Mary Ann Ebert (derived from other sources). Used by permission.
7. 'Give thy peace' quoted in *Morning, Noon and Night*, ed. John Carden (London: CMS, 1976).
8. 'Silent before God' from *Discipleship*, compiled and edited by the Hutterian Brethren (Rifton, NY: Plough, 1994).
9. 'The Lord's majesty' from *Confessions* 1.1, trans. R.S. Pine-Coffin (Harmondsworth: Penguin, 1961).
10. 'Prayer at the beginning of the day', adapted from Philaret of Moscow, *A Manual of Eastern Orthodox Prayers* (SPCK). Used by permission.
11. 'All the day long' from 'Wisdom and Innocence' (19 February 1843) in *Sermons Bearing on Subjects of the Day* (1843), no. 20.

Chapter 5

1. 'Make your circle, God' by John Johansen-Berg in *Textures of Tomorrow: Words and Images on the Theme of Reconciliation*, ed. Kate Compston (London: URC, 1996). Used by permission.
2. 'A new world' from *Your Will Be Done* (Singapore: CCA, 1984).
3. 'May anger and fear turn to love' in *An African Prayer Book*, ed. Desmond Tutu. Copyright © 1995 by Desmond Tutu. Used by permission of Doubleday, a division of Bantam Doubleday Dell Publishing Group, Inc. Copyright © Hodder and Stoughton Limited in the UK and reproduced by permission of the publishers.
4. 'A North American prayer' from a special service of 'Intercession for the Summit' to support the urban gang leaders' meeting in Kansas City in 1993.
5. 'When our love is torn or battered' by Andrew Pratt © 1997 Stainer & Bell Ltd, London, England, from *Blinded by the Dazzle*. Used by permission.
6. 'Hand in hand' by Beena Sebastian, from the International Fellowship of Reconciliation's Women Peacemakers Program. Used by permission.
7. 'God is not far from my people' from *The Calvary of My People: The Gospel Alive in El Salvador* (London: PRAXIS, n.d.).
8. 'Like Aaron's staff' from *Faith of a People* (Maryknoll NY: Orbis Books). Used by permission.

Chapter 6

1. 'Say 'No' to peace', Brian Wren © 1986 Stainer & Bell Ltd for the world except USA, Canada, Australia and New Zealand. Reprinted from *Peace Together Praise* and used by permission.
2. 'Nobody's business' from *A Testament of Hope: The Essential Writings of Martin Luther King, Jr*, ed. James M. Washington (New York: Harper & Row, 1986).

3. 'In place of a curse' from *Your Will Be Done* (Singapore: CCA, 1984). Used by permission.
4. 'Talk to us', copyright © Claretian Communications Inc, Quezon City, MM, Philippines. Used by permission.
5. 'Poem of an angry person' from *Your Will Be Done* (Singapore: CCA, 1984).
6. 'Peace that passes understanding' from *Prayers of the Way*, copyright © Methodist Publishing House, Peterborough, UK. Used by permission.

Chapter 7

1. 'Peace and conflict' by Hugh Montefiore in *Theology* (July 1998).
3. 'Cleansing the temple' © 1991 Mary Ann Ebert. Used by permission.
4. 'A new heart', from a prayer card used by the Amnesty International Religious Bodies Liaison Panel. Used by permission.
5. 'Why have you forsaken me?' from *Psalms* (London: Sheed & Ward, 1981).
6. 'Your peace' by Dom Helder Camara, *The Desert is Fertile* (London: Sheed & Ward, 1974).
7. 'Armed struggle' from *El Salvador: A Spring Whose Waters Never Run Dry*, ed. Scott Wright et al. (Washington DC: EPICA, 1990).
8. 'Witness of the women' from *All Desires Known*, copyright © Janet Morley 1988, 1992. Reproduced by permission of SPCK and Morehouse Publishing, Harrisburg, PA.
9. 'World of Contradictions' © 1997 Mary Ann Ebert. Used by permission.
10. 'Peace, justice and love of God' from *Catholic Worker*, quoted in Pax Christi UK World Peace Day leaflet.
12. 'Dedication' from *Your Will Be Done* (Singapore: CCA, 1984). Used by permission.

Chapter 8

1. 'God is love', taken from *Into Your Hands* by Dom Helder Camara, published and copyright 1987 by Darton Longman and Todd Ltd and used by permission of the publishers.
2. 'Fear not, stand firm' from *He Is Our Peace: Meditations on Christian Nonviolence* from *The Writings of Howard Goeringer, Eberhard Arnold, Christoph F. Blumhardt, & Others*, ed. Emmy Barth (Plough Publishing House, 1994).
3. 'The power of hope' from *Your Will Be Done* (Singapore: CCA, 1984). Used by permission.
4. 'Peace beyond understanding' from *Lift Thine Eyes: Evening Prayers* by Christoph Blumhardt © 1988 by The Plough Publishing House, Farmington PA, USA. Used with permission.
5. 'A Christmas meditation' from *Why, O Lord? Psalms & Sermons from Namibia* (Geneva: WCC Publications, 1986).
6. 'And the waters will flow from your altar, Lord', reprinted from Ernesto Barros Cardoso, *Whole Life, Holy Life* (Rio de Janeiro, 1993).
7. 'False paths' from *Inner Land: A Guide to the Heart and Soul of the Bible* (Rifton, NY: Plough, 1976).

Chapter 9

2. 'In a small way', published by the International Fellowship of Reconciliation.
3. 'My peace I give unto you', taken from *The Rhymes of G A Studdert Kennedy* © 1940. Reproduced by permission of Hodder and Stoughton Limited.
4. 'Look with compassion' from the Week of Prayer for Christian Unity material 1978 in *For All God's People* (Geneva: WCC Publications, 1978).

128

5. 'Glorious opportunities', quoted in *For All God's People* (Geneva: WCC Publications, 1978).

6. 'The will to be free' from *Your Will Be Done* (Singapore: CCA, 1984).

7. 'Women of this day' from 'Appeal to womanhood throughout the world' (September 1870), text as reproduced by the Baptist Peace Fellowship of North America. Used by permission.

8. 'A paraphrase of the Beatitudes' © W.L. Wallace (Bill), Aotearoa/New Zealand. Used by permission.

9. 'Courage to stand up' from *Instrument of Thy Peace* (London: Fount, 2nd edn 1983).

10. 'The peacemaker's job' quoted in *Baptist Peacemaker* (Spring–Summer 1995).

11. 'Dedication of a peace person' quoted in *Crying Out Loud*, ed. Ann Arthur (London: Unitarian Worship Subcommittee, 1987).

12. 'Step by stumbling step' from *Crying Out Loud*, ed. Ann Arthur (London: Unitarian Worship Subcommittee, 1987). Used by permission.

13. 'Working for justice' from *Thanksgiving 5, A Prayer Book for Australia* (Broughton Books, 1995).

14. 'Take… and make' from *Textures of Tomorrow: Words and Images on the Theme of Reconciliation*, ed. Kate Compston. Published by the United Reformed Church, 1996. Used by permission.

Chapter 10

1. 'Be born in us', Susan Brittion, Durban, South Africa, 1997. Used by permission.

2. 'Web of peace' from *Leaves from the Tree of Peace: A Resource Book of Words and Pictures*, ed. John P. Reardon. Published by the United Reformed Church © 1986. Used by permission.

3. 'Lord of peace' from *Lift Thine Eyes: Evening Prayers* by Christoph Blumhardt © 1988 by The Plough Publishing House, Farmington PA, USA. Used with permission.

4. 'Embrace' by Rubem A. Alves, University of Campinas, São Paulo, taken from *Edged with Fire: Prayer Handbook 1994*, ed. Kate Compston (London: URC, 1994).

5. 'I beg to differ' from *Your Will Be Done* (Singapore: CCA, 1984).

6. 'The shadow of the dove' by Kate McIlhagga, *The Pattern of Our Days: Liturgies and Resources for Worship*. The Iona Community (Wild Goose Publications, Glasgow, 1996). Used by permission.

7. 'Outstretched hands' quoted in *Textures of Tomorrow: Words and Images on the Theme of Reconciliation*, ed. Kate Compston (London: URC, 1996).

8. 'Gifts' by Kate McIlhagga in *Textures of Tomorrow: Words and Images on the Theme of Reconciliation*, ed. Kate Compston (London: URC, 1996). Used by permission.

9. 'God is weaving' © Yvonne Dahlin. Used by permission.

10. 'Psalm 23' in *Why, O Lord? Psalms & Sermons from Namibia* by Zephania Kameeta © 1986 WCC Publications, World Council of Churches, Geneva, Switzerland. Used by permission.

11. 'The sending forth' by Mary Ann Ebert (derived from other sources). Used by permission.